Kidmin REFORMATION

A NO-NONSENSE LOOK AT DISCIPLING THE NEXT GENERATION

TORNADO TWINS

Kidmin Reformation:
A No-Nonsense Look at Discipling the Next Generation

by Tornado Twins

Trade paperback ISBN: 978-1-943294-49-7
Ebook ISBN: 978-1-943294-50-3

Cover design by Tornado Twins

Published by Kidmin Nation

Kidmin Reformation is also available on Amazon Kindle, Barnes & Noble Nook and Apple iBooks.

Contents

INTRODUCTION

"Let me show you our church so you understand why we're atheists." —Sebastian, age 15

Sebastian was just a kid—young, blond, only 15 years old. But when he looked up at my twin brother and me, the fierce expression in his eyes had the look of someone older. A brisk Norwegian wind blew through his hair. His friends, all kids or teenagers, stood around him, evidence that they also stood with him, united in thought and purpose. Clearly, they all had a plan.

"We're going to show you our town," Sebastian said to us. "We'll start by going *there*." His finger pointed across a cold river to a building that looked to be well over a hundred years old. It was a church. *The* church of the town. The peak of its spire jutted skyward high above the beautiful landscape.

As we started to walk in its direction, he added, "First—we'll go to the church to show you why we are atheists." His friends nodded in agreement.

I felt as if a bomb had gone off inside me. Sebastian's words exploded in my heart. I wasn't responsible for this church or any of its history; nonetheless, I was stung with conviction. The deeper meaning behind his statement kept repeating over and over again in my heart as we followed our young Norwegian guides to the old edifice: *We want to share with you who we are. So let me show you our church so you understand why we're atheists.*

My brother, Efraim, and I had stopped in Norway while visiting Europe to do a YouTube meet-up. About ten kids had gathered to meet us who were, as it's called, our YouTube "fans." These kids were among our earliest YouTube subscribers and had been with us ever since, following our posts for more than four years. They had joined us back when we had only 100 subscribers—about 70,000 less than we have today. Sebastian was 11 back then.

We'd been in contact with this group off and on and developed a great friendship with them and their families. After flying to Europe for vacation and business, we rerouted our trip on the way back so we could meet them. They invited us into their homes and showed us the typical Norwegian traditions. We taught them some English and showed them how to develop videogames.

But that was later in the meet-up. Our first meeting was with Sebastian and his friends—and the first thing they wanted to show us was their church (especially their disgust of it). They knew we followed Jesus and they were not against that. Not at all, actually. What they were against was the fact that they themselves had no access to Jesus. Not through the church, at least.

I don't want to make it sound as if the church in their town was "bad." It wasn't. Actually, it was great—but only for the oldest generation. It hadn't adjusted to being relevant to the youngest generation. Sure, there were programs for kids and youth, but none spoke the kids' language. As a result, these guys felt no love from the church—and in their hearts, at least, they had abandoned it.

Efraim and I were shocked not just by what Sebastian had said but also by *when* he'd said it. We'd only just said hi! Immediately they wanted to take us to their church. It was the *first* thing they wanted to do after we met. They could've taken us to the ski slopes first or to get some authentic Norwegian food or to the icy-cold river (from which they later showed us how to drink). But this group of kids decided to show us their church.

If we'd taken at face value what Sebastian said, we'd have misunderstood these kids. They described their church in explicit terms, and it would have been easy for us to conclude that they were hostile to the church, that atheism had taken hold in their hearts. But the church was the *first* thing they wanted to show us about their town. This was no attempt at mockery. This was a spiritual cry. They were saying: "Why don't we have what you have? We want to know Christ, but the door is closed to us. And we're ticked off about it!"

In this small story is a big lesson for us. We often think that only those inside the church can question or disapprove of where the church is headed. But the church is for everybody, and sometimes the atheists outside our walls intuitively know the church isn't being obedient to Christ. Sometimes their plea for change is 100 percent correct. Even if they're only 15 years old.

Sadly, for these kids the church doors had been closed to them their entire lives. Still, it had quite a hold on their local youth culture, requiring kids to go through "confirmation," a religious rite of passage. Kids being confirmed would have to publicly proclaim that they believed in God. Sebastian told me he'd made the proclamation.

"But I don't believe in God," he said. "I just lied. Yes, I lied in church. But don't worry about it; it's just tradition."

And he was right. The church experience for him and other kids was just tradition. Nothing more. No connection with God, no talking back and forth with your Maker, no learning how God Himself whispers His purpose into each day, giving your life meaning.

In America we believe we're so much better off. We tend to think, *Some churches may be headed toward tradition, but luckily we're not like the ones in Europe!* We hear this phrase all the time. *Newsflash:* We're already like Europe. We're just a few years behind in the process.

A quick study of history will show you that Europe already had its megachurch movement. Europe already had the majority-Christian society who then lost their majority position. In America we often think we're above it all. But we aren't. We're just operating a little behind European Christianity in time. When you fly to Europe, you're flying ahead in time when it comes to the spiritual progression society there has taken. We'd be much wiser to learn from Europe than to say how "dark things are over there," while feeling superior.

In *your* future, which kids will point at your church building and say, "Let us show you why we're atheists?" In fact, which kids are already doing so now? You know they're out there, and maybe their cry isn't that sacrilegious. They wish to enter, but they are growing up speaking another language, a language the church refuses to learn. And, therefore, the door is closed to them. Our door. Your door.

THERE'S GOOD NEWS

There's a lot of good news in Europe. Some churches fully understand the postmodern culture, and they're growing fast. When you look at the historical timeline, you see that the Church in Europe firs had to be stripped of its riches and pride before it was finally willing to change.

The question is: are we willing to change as well?

My brother and I have grown up while being a part of one of these incredible church movements in Europe. Our church paid the price for change because many other churches didn't always understand ours. But this price did not compare with the joy God gave us. He used our church to reach kids and youth nobody was reaching. Families changed. People got off drugs. People's lives filled with meaning. Harsh characters changed into loving people. Fathers and children reconciled. Broken families came together again. The joy was constant. The harvest was plentiful. The meaning was deep.

The Church of America—like any Church around the world—is now faced with a choice. Do we keep thinking we have it all together, or will we follow where God is leading? Because where He's leading is so, so good! You don't want to miss out by settling for your current successes.

I long for the day when kids will point at your church and say, "Let us show you why we follow Christ."

On the last day of our stay in Norway we climbed the ski slope. There was no snow just yet, and we sat down together looking over the town they called home. One of the boys began to tell us how he'd always been curious about the Bible and how grateful he was that he met us. I showed him videos of what our church was like, and he said, "If this existed in Norway, I'd come every week."

When we dropped the kids off that day, this boy—his name was Sander—was the last to be dropped off. We asked if we could pray for his life, and his eyes lit up like we were offering him a gift better than any he'd ever received. We prayed that Jesus would enter his life and fill each of his days with meaning, and that God would use him to be a spiritual Viking—yes, we had to throw the Viking part in there—bringing God's meaning wherever he went.

After we prayed for him, he was quiet for a long time, and then let out a deep long sigh. It was like he exhaled the worries of this world—he had found what he was looking for, and his journey toward Christ had started. He wanted to take a picture so that he would not forget the moment.

Later that day we saw that he'd posted it on social media, saying it was the best day of his life—ever.

By the way, we sent this Introduction to Sebastian. After reading it, he told us that it describes exactly how he felt. "Wow, it's really true," he said. Then we asked him if he had a message for America's church and youth ministry leaders. Here's what he said:

"Be wise, listen to the twins, because church in Norway is the most boring thing we know of."

In our experience, the term "boring" is what kids use when the door is closed for them. Sebastian then asked if all church leaders wear the traditional hats his town's clergy wear. We told him no. (He joked that we should tell all of them that they should! So there, we kept our promise.)

This is the work you and I are called to do. To show kids like Sebastian what's true about God, to lead kids like Sander to the best days of their lives—and to lead them all to meet and walk with their Maker. They can follow Him in whatever cultural context, whatever "language" they choose.

But are we willing to change in order to learn their language? If we hope to reach kids like Sebastian, Sander, and their friends, then, as children's and family ministry leaders, we must be willing to go through a reformation in our own churches, to face what we aren't doing right and let it go, to embrace what we are doing right and strengthen it, to climb out of our ruts and let God do something new. If we will do this, then we will see kids' lives changed and families transformed with the Gospel.

Good news!

That's what this book is all about: to help you experience a kidmin reformation in your own ministry. On these pages you'll learn how the secular world sees the church and how to adjust to this rising view, which children's ministry traditions are holding you back and how to deal with them, paradigm-shifts that will radically change your ministry, which biblical methods will improve your ministry's God-given effectiveness, and a whole lot more.

Ready for the Reformation? Let's get to it then!

—Ruben and Efraim Meulenberg

Part 1

THE TIME FOR SMALL-TALK IS OVER

Chapter 1
ALL IS WELL (OR IS IT?)

CAN I BE BRUTALLY HONEST? You're a busy person so I'd rather skip the small talk and get right to a vital point that this book addresses.

Here goes:

The Church today is not doing well when it comes to the next generation.

Whew. I'm glad that's out. Did that sound negative? Think before you answer because, well, here comes another point:

The Church today is not doing well when it comes to children's ministry.

Now, before you think I'm setting you up for the most depressing writing you've ever read about kidmin, let me assure you, I'm not. On the contrary, I'm all about solutions to these issues. And there are quite a bunch of them, in fact. In this book I'm going to show you what they are and how to implement them in your own ministry. But I would be doing you a disservice if I were to begin with the solutions without first laying out a picture of the things that are broken.

Once we get to the solutions, this book will rapidly list many solutions needed for our day and age. It will go really fast, because

I value your time. We've all read the books that just drone on about a certain subject and never get to the meat of things.

But before that—in the first few chapters—we investigate what's going on in our current era of children's ministry. These chapters will both encourage you and break your heart. They'll strip away the many incorrect ideas that are floating around in kidmin, and they will fortify you so that you won't burn out once you're implementing the countless new ideas in the rest of the book.

Didn't Nehemiah take a good survey of the broken walls of Jerusalem before he set out to rebuild them? He was in deep grief over the condition of his city, and so am I about children's ministry. But it didn't start off that way for me. I once believed it all was great. And why wouldn't I have? I mean, look around—we have more beautiful materials than ever, we go to wonderful conferences, our children's ministries look like mini-Disneylands, and when senior pastors look down the halls of their churches they nod their heads and think: *It's all great down the hall in the children's ministry. Ours is loved by kids and families. Man, I think it might even be an example for the entire nation.*

With a wonderful mixture of joy and pride about their kidmins, the pastors continue their ministry to the adults, not bothering to go down to the children's area much anymore. No need to; the kid-thing is covered.

All is well in the children's ministry, they think. *Best of all, parents are happy! Heck, they even chose to attend our church for the quality of our kids ministry. Praise the Lord, it's all peachy. All peachy.*

CRUMBLING WALLS

I've worked at numerous megachurches, and at many of them I hosted visiting pastors for tours around the church campus. They'd come from around the globe came to see how our church did it. It was like being in Jerusalem at the height of Solomon's reign! Visitors would come from all over the planet! They'd be so impressed with our facilities. They'd take notes. They'd grab all the literature they could, whatever we had lying around. They'd take pictures. They'd ask questions, and we'd answer them. And they would leave deeply touched.

During their visits, I would be deeply moved too—but not like they were. Because I was dying inside. God made sure of that. I can hear you now: *God made sure you were dying inside?* Yes. He wouldn't let me have the fake joy. And I didn't want it. Because beneath the veneer, underneath that happy outward appearance of impressive kids ministries, I knew we weren't living in Solomon's era at all. We were in Nehemiah's era, when the walls of Jerusalem lay crumbled, the Temple had collapsed, and across the land God's people were defenseless. I was seeing the same thing, not just in our children's ministry, but also throughout the nation and around the world.

Okay, okay, I can hear you. You're saying: "Now, hold on, Mr. Gloomy. That's a pretty broad and bleak assessment of the Church, the nation, and the world. How did you come to such a dismal conclusion?"

Fair question. It all started when I read a blog post about the state of the church. It rocked my world. And today I thank God it did.

A VISION IN THE NIGHT

That blogger compared fourteen separate research reports. Each one studied kids that grew up with church as part of their upbringing. The most positive report found that more than 40 percent of kids leave the Church before they turn 18, compared with the least positive one, which placed the figure at 88 percent. The average landed at a perfect 75 percent.

Being an optimistic guy I immediately dismissed the findings. I mean, the blogger wasn't well-known anyway. And how many so-called Christians yell scary things online? Come on, I have enough trouble sifting through the nonsense that my Facebook friends post. How much more some random blogger whom I don't know?

Let's just trust God, shall we? If God's on our side, then what could possibly—

Lord, why don't you take this eerie feeling away? Why don't you allow my heart to just let this go? What is it Lord? Aarrgh.

As I wrestled with my inner turmoil, trying to happily continue the ministry work I'd been given, God wouldn't let me go. HE had made the point for me, not the blog post. And he kept at it. It became for me like a holy frustration. A thorn in the flesh. Or, as *The Matrix* calls it, a splinter in the brain.

One night, while I was tossing and turning unable to sleep, the thorn was creating mental visions. I pictured 75 percent of our kids leaving. The kids I'd come to love. They silently slipped out while their satisfied parents smiled at me, thumbs up, loving the good job we were doing. But their kids were walking away, not speaking a word. They were turning their backs on the Church. Embracing the shadows, being enveloped by the darkness. Nobody was seeing it, though. Not even the parents. They were just happy with the ministry. That's what counted most. They didn't see the exodus going on all around them. But I could see it. And, again, I felt like I was dying inside. I couldn't take the idea that what I was seeing was real.

The next morning I decided to take a deeper look at the fourteen reports. Some were churchwide studies. You know, Barna-type stuff. Others were the result of deep research of specific denominations. All of them were legit. I'd never been sick because of an idea. But, I confess, I was physically ill for a good week. Call me an emotional guy—and you'd be right, actually—but when God's messing with your heart, what do can you do? I was a wreck.

HALF SAVED = HALF LOST

During that week I discovered one point of light. Another blog. It gave me a glimmer of hope.

It claimed that the number of kids leaving church was not entirely complete because, as the writer argued, around 30 percent of those kids would return to the Church after they had kids of their own. I checked out the data, and it too seemed legit, like the fourteen other studies. The writer was correct in many cases.

Ignoring the fact that these "returners" would also make some of their most important life decisions while away from the Church, such as whom to marry, what jobs to choose, where to live, this report was at least a bit more hopeful.

Still, even with the delayed uptick, it means we will lose 45 percent of the people. Our own people. Those who have grown up in our own churches. You see, any organization that loses 45 percent of its people would be considered an epic failure. Sure, you've retained roughly half of what you once had. But you've also lost almost half!

Let's say you have two kids. At that rate, you'll lose one. If you have four, you'll lose two. Statistically speaking, of course. And it would never happen to your family, right?

Right?

As I was going through what felt like 3,000 phases of grief and confusion, I still wasn't convinced that such a tremendous number of kids were turning into the walking dead. For some reason, I'm much more eager to accept happy numbers and dismiss negative ones. (Is anybody else reading this like me?). Surely if the epic magnitude of this exodus were even remotely true, every children's minister everywhere would know. They'd all be aware of it, and therefore solutions would be readily available.

So I decided to attend a large, national children's ministry conference. I wanted to hang with the leaders, the gurus, the experts. Sure, I'd hung out with many of these guys and gals for years. I was part of the club. But this time I decided not to contact anyone to let them know I was coming. I'd go in quietly. Just be an observer. A learner. No backstage talks. No meet 'n' greets or grip 'n' grins in the green room. No group selfies. No networking. Just learning—in quiet humility.

I walked alone into the big meeting room and sat down for the first session. With a sigh and a heavy heart, I lifted up a prayer. "Okay, God, hit me."

Chapter 2

COMING FACE TO FACE WITH THE PROBLEM

WORD TO THE WISE: if you ever pray, "God, hit me," then get ready for your world to be rocked. He "hits" a lot harder than you might think He will. But always in love, and always to move you to action.

So maybe I should take that back—go ahead, say that prayer and mean it: "God, hit me!" Because when God "slaps" you across the face, your life will never be the same.

So, can you guess when God answered my prayer? Well, it wasn't during worship. (Sorry, I've been singing the same praise songs for years. Yeah, I know, it's all been for God; but He's the one who told us to sing Him "a new song" [Ps. 96:1]). Okay, let's get back on point.)

He didn't hit me by saying something through the main speaker either. In fact, the keynote speaker hadn't even come onstage yet.

FEELING THE STING OF DRY EYES

God hit me—now, don't laugh—during the sponsored message that played smack (no pun intended) at the beginning of the session. He used a *commercial break* to speak to me! The jumbotron footage showed pictures of children, and then a voice rattled off some statistics and firmly stated, "The church in America loses 75 percent of kids before they turn 18."

Wham!

Right across the face. The "slap" of the Spirit actually stung my heart, not my face.

OK, God, you didn't waste any time there, did you?

I know it's biblical and all, but the last thing I wanted to do was turn the other cheek!

Memories of the kids I serve each week raced through my brain. Tears filled my eyes. Defenseless and out for the count, I looked around the room. I looked at my fellow children's workers. Surely they felt the same sting I was feeling.

Would there be outrage?

Would they be shocked?

Would I suddenly see tears?

No. None. I saw none of that at all. They all nodded like a Church in agreement: "Yes pastor." "Good word, pastor." My jaw dropped. Everybody already knew the sad stat that was causing my emotional earthquake!

"IDLE" WORSHIP IN THE CAMP?

My inner 5-year-old threw a tantrum. "How am I always the last one in the know?" I whined. "Fifteen years of children's ministry, and I'm the last one to hear this?" I felt like the sibling who discovers the candy bag when there's only one piece left. You know, that kind of "late." (Okay, we're using candy illustrations now. This is getting real serious. But yeah, it's that important).

Then the ad continued, saying that because of this terrible phenomenon, you should really use their curriculum. Why, the ad asked? Because they've been the biggest, baddest, and most-trusted curriculum for over thirty years. Everybody cheered. "We use it!" people yelled. "It's great!"

I felt like I was in a movie, like I had landed in *Toy Story* and we all were the green guys worshiping the claw. No deep soul-searching was happening in that room. Instead, we were collectively reaffirming our devotion to the altar of Doing It the Same Way We've Been Doing It the Last Thirty Years.

And that would be because those thirty years have been so effective, right?

Excuse my sarcasm—of course it makes total sense to continue with what's been working so well. Only 25 percent well. Or 75 percent not well at all.

Chapter 3

A BRIGHTLY LIT PIT (IS STILL A PIT)

I LEFT THAT CONFERENCE DISCOURAGED. At times, I had the urge to toss the tables, like Jesus did at the Temple. Two friends who were with me shared the same sentiment. We joked that the next time we had a booth at a children's conference, we'd turn all our furniture upside down. I wondered if we were alone in what we felt or if others were equally distressed about this situation.

When Elijah was discouraged and thought he was the only one serving God, the Lord showed him there were 7,000 others still faithful to Him. That moment marked the start of a God-inspired revolution of change across the land.

Over the next year I had conversations with more than 2,000 children's workers around the globe—and the conversation is still growing. I learned that, luckily, many people aren't like the ones in that meeting room. Many desire change. If you are one of those (one of us!) then I encourage you to let that desire grow into hunger, into desperation, into a God-given appetite to reach our own children again as well as the kids around the world who aren't even close to being reached. Thankfully, in addition to the many conversations I had also found organizations, such as Kidmin Nation, led by people who are more interested in discovering a new future in children's ministry than preserving their past years of experience.

Most of us are aware that something needs to happen. We clearly see symptoms of disease in the body of Christ. Things aren't very healthy in the Next Generation Department. We're telling ourselves positive stories to keep ourselves going—while we wait for the change to come, while we wait for God to do something new.

It's like we've all fallen into a pit and we're painting the walls instead of trying to climb out. The inside of the pit is bright with all kinds of Disney-style colors. But it's still a pit. That's today's children's ministry. And we can't blame ourselves for making it this way because we're just trying to make do with what we have. We do the best we can with the little we've been entrusted with. But that "little" is about to become a whole lot bigger. Why? Because many of us aren't satisfied with staying inside the colorful pit. We want to climb up, toward the light, and move on. We want to make strong disciples of Christ, not play church.

In order to climb out of the pit, we need solutions. But before we move on to the solutions, there are two key issues I need to address.

First, we need to discuss the "parent argument," or Parent Trap. Second, we need to know how we can deal with the depressing statistics related to kids leaving the Church. We all want to see those numbers turned around, but the task is big and we need to know how to handle it without burning out.

The first issue will lead into the second, so let's start with the Parent Trap.

Part 2

LET'S FACE THE REAL-LIFE ISSUES

Chapter 4
THE PARENT TRAP

THE PARENT ARGUMENT, or what we're calling the Parent Trap, goes like this: "You can't blame the children's ministry for kids leaving the Church. The spiritual responsibility lies with the parents."

Don't be tripped up by the "trap." We need to own our faults. The argument is 99 percent valid and 100 percent true—but it doesn't lead to a solution, does it?

Yes, the parents are responsible for the spiritual welfare of their children. God gave them authority over their kids. But we can't, therefore, fall into the Parent Trap and think that whenever things go bad with kids we can just shrug our shoulders and say, "Not my job. Take care of it, Mom. Take care of it, Dad."

Of course, neither can we take on a responsibility that isn't ours. God gives us the strength to do only what He calls us to do; we can't take on the calling of the parents, too. But we *can* be a catalyst for change. We *can* be the beginning of a movement. As we'll talk about later, it's not that hard to be just that.

I once talked with a woman in children's ministry who was the assistant to the children's pastor of the 25th largest church in America. In our casual conversation she proudly talked about her son being "into" Jesus. In my blissful ignorance I asked when her son had accepted Christ. The smile suddenly disappeared from her face. She said she didn't know if he'd ever accepted Christ. Then she proceeded to tell me: "We leave that up to you guys, the children's ministry."

"You guys"?

Hmm. So here was a mom who was delegating the spiritual salvation of her son to the children's ministry, even though she was in children's ministry herself!

See the paradox? We live in a world where parents tend to tell the Church, "*You* take care of them." And the Church tells the parents, "No, *you* take care of them." Kids are like hot potatoes: the parents toss them to the Church—*ooh, ooh, ooh!* the Church bobbles them from hand to hand—and the Church tosses them back.

WE NEED TO SERVE KIDS' FAMILIES

Although this problem exists globally, it's worse in America than in a place like Europe, for example. In America there's this popular saying that it "takes a village" to raise kids. This saying means that it takes many different people—parents, uncles, aunts, churches, good friends, a wonderful community—to be influencers in kids' lives.

Although the original intent of this phrase is true, it has derailed many families because parents take it out of context. It's often used as an excuse to delegate their spiritual responsibility to others. They'll say: "It takes a village, the Church is the spiritual part of that village, so have at it. I'm out!"

And that is how you, the children's worker, end up with what in America is known as the "helicopter parent." This is a Mom or Dad who works overtime to keep good people in their kids' worlds but neglects to have bold, direct conversations themselves with their kids.

Each culture has its own issues in this area. In Western Europe, for example, the common idea in parents' minds is: "I can't choose my kids' path. I can't instill values in them; it has to be their own choice. If I influence them spiritually, it's manipulation."

Kids who grow up in these families are given everything they need, except spiritual food. Because somehow, it's believed, spiritual values cannot be passed on without manipulation. So the kids grow up in a spiritual vacuum. They're spiritually starving. They attend church but they don't get their parents' faith at home, and ultimately can't connect why faith matters to their parents. This leads them to question why it should ever matter to them. And at that point, in swoops atheism.

This isn't a condition isolated to America or Europe. Anywhere you go around the globe, you'll be fighting erroneous ideas in your local culture. And I commend you if you are doing so! We children's ministers can't serve just the kids; we must serve the entire family. If, as a minister, your influence can help a parent to raise their kid in a biblical way, you might find out tomorrow that you helped that child more than if you'd given him a lifetime of children's services.

NO FINGER-POINTING ALLOWED

Ultimately, it's not about pointing fingers at who's responsible. For you, it's about doing what God called you to do. If you're a parent, you're called to parent—all the way. If you're a children's minister, you're called to do anything in your power to give kids and families every opportunity to become disciples of Christ. It's that simple. And each of those callings could mean going way beyond merely holding children's services. Or they may not. It depends on the calling.

In our case, for example, we've been able to set up services that draw kids from all around our area and teach parents how to raise kids spiritually. We're even having a positive influence on kids' massive intake of media by developing movies, video games, and stories that build them up.

So, to conclude the parent argument: yes, it's the parent's responsibility to teach their kids spiritual truth—but where's the change going to start? Will it start with the parents or with the children's ministry? It could be either. But it's most likely going to start with the Church.

So what is your choice? Here's mine: as long as I'm alive, the change is going to start with me. I will affect change in my area of responsibility.

And the same can go for you: as long as you're drawing breath, let the change start with you—in your area of responsibility. That's your calling and your choice.

This leads us to the second point we need to deal with before heading into the solutions.

Chapter 5

STAYING ON-FIRE WITHOUT BURNING OUT

CAUSING CHANGE IN OUR respective ministry areas will require much responsibility from each of us. So how will you and I keep from burning out? Knowing these eerie statistics about kids and the Church, and knowing we also need to help parents, how do we strike the right balance?

To start, there are two things you definitely should *not* do.

1. Don't take responsibility for things outside your area of influence. You can't blame yourself for what God did not call you to do. (I know I have!) Talk with your Maker on what your responsibility is—and what it isn't. It's different for everyone.

2. Don't blame the parents for not doing what you could have done. You don't have to stand before God after your life and say, "Well, it was the parents' responsibility, Lord. So I just kept doing what I always did. I didn't let You break my heart. I didn't increase my love for kids and families. I didn't see the sign of the times and didn't do everything You called me to do to make a change."

In addition to these, simply don't panic!

AVOID FRANTIC PANIC

One way you can know you're in God's plan for your life is by checking your heart. If it's broken for kids but not stressed out, then you're probably right where God wants you. You're following where God leads, *in love,* not in panic, not in desperation. God doesn't lead you onto a road of frantic panic. He doesn't make you say: "I gotta, I gotta, I gotta! Come on, people; kids are dying. Come on, people, *why aren't you with me?*"

Frantic panic means you're working in your own strength. It also makes it really hard for people to want to work alongside you. At the same time, you can be deeply convicted of the dire situation you're seeing, yet follow God in peace on His unforced road of love. That's the kind of heart I encourage you to have as we head into the solutions.

Part 3

MOVING OUT OF THE PIT AND INTO THE LIGHT

Chapter 6

GOD WANTS TO DO SOMETHING NEW

TO SUMMARIZE KEY POINTS we've made so far, there are two healthy phases that we, as leaders in children's ministry, need to go through:

First, rather than turning away from these sickening statistics, we need to allow for a period when we let them sink in. This is a time of grief: *"For in much wisdom is much grief, and he who increases knowledge increases sorrow"* (Eccl. 1:18, NKJV). This period of grief is needed to change us, and to prepare our hearts for God's incoming change. It's not meant to cause you to panic and run ahead in your own strength.

Second, after this period of grief, we need to rededicate ourselves to Christ. Tell Him: "This ministry is Yours, not mine. I am Yours, not mine. Do with this ministry as You please and do with me as You please. I'm ready and available to do as You wish. Since I serve You, this is not my problem. It's Yours. And I'm ready to join You in whatever solution You provide. You've opened my heart, now open my eyes."

What if you prayed that right now, before we head into the solutions?

Done?

Okay, it's time for solutions! Welcome to Opportunityland, where it's bright and sunny! You know, we could have started our book right here, skipping all the cloudy stuff. But our goal was not to write a book with a warm and sunny outlook only; one that would inspire people to cheer for us and then invite us to speak at conferences.

Our goal with this book is to end up with readers who truly wish to make a difference—and to filter out the people who are truly moved, who truly care about the state of children in our time. You'll need passion and strength like that if you want to make the God-given changes that lead to his bountiful harvest. Ministers without that passion simply jump from one new idea to the next, never truly sticking with one, never truly seeking—or seeing—the growth God has in mind.

But since you're still here, still reading, and since you stuck with me through all the book of Lamentations stuff in the previous chapters, it's safe to say that you're one of those change-makers! So let's get to it!

(By the way, sometimes I'll write "I" and sometimes "us." No, I don't do that because I have multiple personalities, if that's what you're thinking! I say "we" and "us" because I'm talking about me and my twin brother, Efraim. And sometimes "us" refers to our team at KidsWantAnswers.com. Okay, I hear you—I'm moving on now!)

God has incredible solutions in mind for today's children's ministry. We're eager to tell you of the ones God has given us and the incredible effect they've had. None of what we will share with you is theory, wishful thinking, or a series of "We shoulds." It's all based on our experience, after doing ministry across three continents.

I'll quickly go over our story. I think you'll find it encouraging. After that, we'll look at the principles that brought about these positive changes, and we'll look at how you can easily implement them in your own ministry.

Chapter 7

THE SOMETHING NEW GOD DID IN US

I WAS 14 WHEN I BEGAN to serving in children's ministry. I was part of a small church in Holland, a few miles from Amsterdam. I was too young to serve, but they needed volunteers, so I slid right in—and I loved it. You could say that I lived for the weekend! But not in the usual Amsterdam way, if you know what I mean. (Make a Note: Most longtime children's ministers started in their teenage years. So go ahead, recruit those wild and crazy teens! You might kick-off a lifelong ministry!) When I turned 17, the children's pastor moved on to other responsibilities, and I was asked to lead the ministry after him. It made no sense that I was chosen. Many people in the church had served much longer than I had. They were older and more experienced. But the cool thing is, they, the leaders with more experience, were the ones who picked me. They felt that a young leader would be good for the church. It was an extremely humble choice on their part. They sacrificed their authority to a young pup; to a kid who had grown up in *their* ministry!

CHALLENGED BY CHANGE

This new responsibility weighed heavily on me. I wanted to do it right. I read every book I could (most came from America) and attended every conference possible. But I felt that none of the resources I was finding would truly connect with the kids we were called to reach. The European materials were 50 years behind at best, and even though the American stuff looked incredible, it wasn't suited for the deeply postmodern Amsterdam culture.

*(**Make a note:** European culture is about twenty years ahead of American culture in postmodernism. Darwinism began in England, and modern atheism more or less fanned out from Germany.)*

What's more, the American materials had not been developed with non-English-speakers in mind and posed too many translation problems. And trying to get million-dollar Christian publishers to change that isn't a thing that 17-year-olds do. We actually did try to get translation deals going after we turned 18, but they kindly dismissed us and wished us the best after telling us they cared so much for "dark, dark Europe." (OK, I don't sound bitter, do I?)

In the meantime, twelve of my fifteen volunteers had left the children's ministry, and stories began to spread that this 17-year-old had no idea what he was doing; that he was running the ministry into the ground. But in reality, I had dismissed the twelve volunteers because they had been guilt-tripped them into staying on. So I told them they didn't have to fulfill the season if God hadn't called them to. They thanked me, and left right away. But it was a good change, because leaders whose hearts aren't in the ministry end up hurting it. The effect of the twelve leaving was positive. Like we'd broken the glass ceiling. The lid was off. We could grow again.

Since we couldn't find good materials, there was only one was forward for us. We had only one choice. Produce our own. (Boy, we had *no* idea how much work we were taking on. But ignorance is bliss sometimes!) We decided to end our youth-ministry services and asked the teenagers to serve in the children's ministry instead, which most agreed to do.

Talk about an integration with youth ministry! Together with those teenagers, we developed the children's programs. During vacation weeks, we'd all serve full time, crafting the programs. Yes, children's programs designed by teenagers. And, boy, did they have a great effect! Within no time our children's ministry had doubled. It became the buzz of the town and if we were to write the stories of lives that were changed, one chapter wouldn't be enough.

*(**Make a note:** We have a training resource on ten things you can do to spread the story of your children's ministry, making it the talk of the town. It's called* 10 Ways to Explode Your Weekend Services. *You'll find it on our website,* KidsWantAnswers.com*).*

LEARNING A LESSON ABOUT CURRICULUM

So before we knew it, churches in the area were asking for our materials, so we'd ship them out to anyone who asked for them. Our story spread like wildfire. Soon we had to charge for the materials because we were sending out so many DVDs. Churches sent back their reports, and many of them were refreshed, doubled in size; some even doubled after doubling!

The growth was exponential, but so were the stories of lives changed. It was then that we learned a valuable lesson: one of the greatest obstacles to highly effective children's ministry is curriculum. You can learn all kinds of principles and try to implement them in your ministry, but if your curriculum isn't written with the same philosophy, it will have zero effect. Your own expertise will always be limited by your curriculum.

All the ongoing problems—kids who don't pay attention, older kids who lose interest, lives that aren't changed, handouts that never make it home—they all can be solved with the correct programs. The problem is not your lack of skill. It's not your lack of training. But if your curriculum doesn't "fit," then it will have the same effect on your ministry as wearing shoes that are too small will have on your feet. Pain will happen.

Growth will stop. Sores won't heal. Worst of all, you'll be at risk of getting used to it and calling it normal. You don't want that!

Within three years, our programs had become the fastest-growing children's curriculum in our language. It was so new that we even experienced a new form of spiritual warfare: Christian publishers! They saw us as a threat that had to be stopped. We were kept out of conferences and experienced smear campaigns (ever heard the word "cult" being used to describe anything new and different?), but nobody could stop what God was doing.

Without any marketing or promotion, the growth kept going. Soon, the Christian publishers changed their form of attack and tried to join forces with us in order to take over control and choke the movement. They met with us in backrooms and told us our materials would sell much better if we "added water to the wine." We responded by saying that Jesus turned *water into wine!*

CALLED TO INTERNATIONAL MINISTRY

After we graduated college, God asked us to let it all go. He wanted to move us into international ministry and needed us to let the ministry go; to let our reputation go; to start over, with nothing, in an unknown land—the United States. We obeyed his call and accepted an offer at a church across the great Atlantic. It would be our first megachurch experience. Not knowing anything about church politics, we had a lot to learn.

We went ahead and implemented bits and pieces of what we'd pioneered in Europe. God blessed the work wherever we went. In the first church, more than 200 kids accepted Christ in less than two months. In other churches we saw a growth of 30 percent in the first two months. We noticed—and please don't take this the wrong way—that ministry in the United States was quite a bit easier than ministry in postmodern Europe. In most cases, secular America still accepts the church as a good thing, whereas in Europe, the church is seen as a group of people who adhere to a dark myth from the past.

The news of our work spread once again. After consulting with churches in the U.S., across Europe, and in Latin America, we discovered again that churches could implement only a limited number of the ideas we presented because their curriculum was holding them back. So we waited for God to give us the green light to produce again. When he did, we started KidsWantAnswers.com.

We were quite nervous because we wanted to do the curriculum really well this time and make it translatable for all languages right from the start (we hadn't forgotten the refusal of the big publishers!). We also wanted to incorporate new media, from film to videogames (you may have heard of our videogame *David* for PC, Mac, and PlayStation) because today's generation of kids is best taught by a multitude of media angles.

KIDSWANTANSWERS.COM (AND SO DID WE!)

Doing all this took quite a bit of capital to start. We had no investors or givers, just some savings. I quit my job at one of the best-known churches in the nation, a potential first step toward career suicide, and began the small ministry that serves children's workers. I prayed for God to show me that I was on the right track, and God said he would.

The very next day an old man came up to me with tears in his eyes. He'd seen KidsWantAnswers.com and said he wanted to contribute to it. He wouldn't let go of my hand, saying that God had told him this ministry would have a great effect, more than we'd know, and faster than we'd expect. He gave me a check of $100. He was our first and only giver. A month later, 750 churches from thirteen nations had signed up. Six months later that number reached 2,000. They all encouraged our work, telling us of the great effects our curriculum was having in their churches.

As I write this, we're about to celebrate our first anniversary of KidsWantAnswers.com. We're working with what we have, while being deeply encouraged by reports from churches that are seeing the same amazing things happen that we've seen. God is on the move and he's doing something new! Can you see it?

Chapter 8

FIRST THINGS FIRST: WHERE TO START

OK, ENOUGH ABOUT OUR STORY. This is about *your* ministry. The reason I told you our story is to show you what's possible in *your* church. Since you too are a change-maker, we know you want to learn how you too can plant these principles in your church and see them spring to life—and, best of all, see Jesus change kids' lives.

But how will that work, exactly?

What changes did God give us that you too can implement? And which of them are ones we *all* need to make before we can take children's ministry from the pit it's in today to the place of purpose God where wants it to be?

We could fill hours' worth of training while answering those questions—and, admittedly, we have!—but for this chapter it would be good to mention the essentials. Ready? Here they are:

There are three areas that each children's ministry needs to address:

1. Your ministry philosophy. Every ministry is based on a philosophy, whether it's verbalized or not. All of our ministry actions are influenced by what we believe. To change, we need to start first by changing our philosophy. ***(Make a note):*** *Change starts in our hearts and minds.*

2. (Re-)training your (volunteer) leaders. When your philosophy changes, your leaders need to be updated. You're taking them with you on the journey. They need to know where you're going and how you plan to get there. Luckily, new information is invigorating to them. They thrive on new vision. Vision is life-giving, and having it protects us from dropping off and dropping out.

(Make a note): *"Where there is no vision, the people perish"* (Prov. 29:18, KJV).

3. Your curriculum. Your curriculum is the blueprint of your weekly programs, and your programs should reflect your philosophy. If you're constantly rewriting the curriculum you're using, then you know it doesn't fit your ministry philosophy. It's that simple. But it goes further than that. The right curriculum can be forward-leaning, giving you results you never knew could happen. Ever heard of kids starting their own small groups? No? It's because it isn't in your curriculum. How about kids leading other kids to Christ rather than only inviting them to church? No? Then it's not in your curriculum. How about, you're *not* the one who teaches the Bible story, but the kids teach themselves? No? Then it's not in your curriculum.

(Make a note): *Vision without implementation is hallucination. And what implements your vision? Your curriculum does. Curriculum is your ministry's blueprint. If it's not in your curriculum, it won't happen!*

Philosophy, Training, Curriculum: Those are the change-makers. The rest of this book will focus on the first and most important one: **a new philosophy**. That's where it all starts. That's where you'll feel invigorated and re-energized.

Our website has plenty of information on the other two (KidsWantAnswers.com).

What follows is a list of all essential changes we made that led to a radically new way of doing children's ministry. What I'm about to describe for you set us decades ahead. Our prayer is that these principles will move children's ministry forward. That they will prompt us to quit painting the walls of the pit and step into Opportunityland, where we can enjoy ministry again and watch God use us in changing people's lives.

Note that these principles work internationally. Not because they are so brilliant, but because they are biblical. Whatever is biblical works everywhere. These essentials aren't about clever systems or methodologies. They're about living out the Bible in ways that the youngest and latest generation can understand.

*(**Make a note:** Every ten years, the youngest generation changes. That means, we need to re-evaluate our ministry methods at least that often!)*

Let's get to it!

Part 4

KIDMIN REFORMATION: HOW IT'S DONE

Chapter 9
RETHINK YOUR MINISTRY

We've finally arrived at the solutions. The rest of this book will take you through the change principles. We've taught these principles around the globe, and have seen dramatic changes. Some principles are practical "how-tos", other principles are on how we should change our thinking, which will lead you to many new practical "how-tos".

Note that the book will pick up speed quite a bit from here on forward. My goal was to give you as many solutions as possible within the length of this book. If you're reading through it in one sitting, you might want to go back to each principle later, and chew on them a bit more... because they'll fly by fast!

Here we go.

Principle No. 1 – Accept that the organized church is now seen as a cultural negative.

This seems like an odd first point, doesn't it? Isn't it bad to accept the fact that the organized church is viewed as a negative in our culture? Why would we ever embrace that viewpoint? Isn't that a terrible thing to believe?

No, it's not. It's crucial, in fact. Postmodernism is rising around the globe, and in a few decades America will be as postmodern as Europe. Don't worry, postmodern culture actually isn't as bad as it's advertised to be—but only if you adjust to it. The best way we can adjust is to humble ourselves. This happens when we accept the truth: that the church is no longer assumed to be an authority. And definitely not *the* authority.

When we embrace this fact, something wonderful happens. Instead of assuming our authority over culture, we become service-oriented. We become humble. We become servants. We explain ourselves better; we suddenly communicate much better with those who aren't part of the church. We have more patience with those who need to be reached. We become less demanding and more loving.

In all our ministry endeavors Efraim and I explain how a life with Christ is beneficial. We don't just expect people to follow our lead because we know what the Bible says. In Europe, all churches that still assume they are an authority are plateaued or dying. Non-Christians view them as judgmental and sour—and from their point of view, they might have a point! Sadly, in the U.S., many churches still get away with assuming their position of authority. Some are even growing. But not for long.

So why do we still wait to make changes in our relationship with our society until secular culture rejects us as no longer good? Read this next sentence carefully: There are *so* many benefits to *not* being the top dog. Let's say that again: *There are so many benefits to not being the top dog.*

Jesus wasn't the top dog. Right?

Herod was. The Pharisees were. Caesar was.

And where are they now? Long gone.

Why? Well, for one, because they didn't embrace Matthew 20:26: *"Whoever wants to be a leader among you must be your servant."*

Principle No. 2 – Make a conscious choice to break with church tradition.

Children's ministry has been around for a while. That means many practices are based on a long legacy of tradition. These traditions worked, once. But they don't connect with kids anymore. Fortunately, it's easy to step away from them. After all, it's much easier for a children's pastor to change his children's ministry than it is for a senior pastor to change his church programs. Why? Because adults resist change, but kids mostly embrace change. That's why children's ministry is the perfect place for church innovation.

One of the pastors we worked for would always start with the children's ministry when he needed to implement a church-wide change. When the innovation took hold, he would turn to the adults and say: "Your kids are already doing this. They've been doing it for over a year now."

It boggles my mind that so many children's ministries are still traditional when kid's ministry instead can be a safe haven for change—a great lab environment for innovation. So let's get to it! Define the traditions that don't work anymore, and break with them. They served their purpose in their time. It's a new time now. Here are five traditional ideas you should break away from. As you know, change starts with our philosophy, and the following five traditions are actually philosophies. They started decades ago and need to be retired if we hope to reach the latest generation:

Disposable Tradition 1: Kids are the church of the future. Kids aren't the church of the future. They *are* the church right *now*! Most curriculums assume that you're preparing kids for a Christian life in the future. I'm sorry, but that's school thinking, not church thinking. You're helping them live their lives with Christ *now*. You're helping them discover their calling at this very moment. You're helping them connect with God on how to live their days for him now, not later!

In fact, kids can be much better at connecting with God than adults are. After all, Jesus told us to "become like a child." Children don't have to obey that command; they already are "like a child"! They already have childlike faith. They have this faith now. They're ready now. They can be Christians now. And, as Jesus said, they can even shame the wisest adults: *"I praise you, Father...because you've hidden these things from the wise and learned, and revealed them to little children"* (Matt 11:25, NIV).

Disposable Tradition 2: We are the teachers, and kids are the learners. Of course, this idea is true to a certain extent because we teach kids and they learn. But it's not complete. Not by far. God speaks through kids as well. Since they *are* the church, we must let them *be* the church. If your children's ministry is all about top-down teaching, kids will check out. It's not just about their learning; it's also about their being the church. It's also about their serving, speaking, and teaching. We'll look at how to accomplish this later.

Disposable Tradition 3: The Aaawwww Effect instead of the Wow Effect. The *Aaawww* Effect is anything that makes adults say, "*Aaawww*!" when they look at kids in your ministry. It's when we treat kids like they're cute kittens in a basket. For the record, kids hate being treated like kittens in a basket. They want to count. They want to matter. They want to make a difference. And you can help them to.

If instead we look for beautiful *aaawww* moments when we can fawn over them, then we're belittling our own kids. Sure, when they're really young they might like that attention and affection because it feels positive and flattering, but when they hit the elementary ages they begin to resist it. And rightfully so.

Sadly, most children's programs focus on this *Aaawww* Effect. I can't open a children's ministry magazine without seeing pictures that are meant to make me say, "*Aaawww!*" Apparently it sells. But it goes further than children's ministry literature. We even serve our own kids a steady diet of teaching videos that were purchased because it made us think, "Oh, how cute for the kids." *Word to the wise:* if any material ever makes you go, "*Aaawww*, how cute for the kids," then I can guarantee that you've lost the elementary-age kids. Kids don't *aaawww*. It's an adult thing. It touches the parent's heart, not the kid's heart. We need to change that style. Fast. But how? Like this: we need to go from *Aaawww* to *Wow!* The Wow Effect is when kids themselves say, "Wow!" The Wow Effect is about what *kids* like, not what *we* like. So maybe we should stop pushing kids into cute choirs or having them rehearse cutesy plays for the adults. These things are meant to make adults feel good, but they don't make disciples of our kids. Trust me, when kids truly follow Christ, it makes their parents feel a lot better than when they watch their kids sing a Christmas carol on stage once a year.

Disposable Tradition 4: Kids can absorb only a finite amount. I can't count the meetings I've had in which the subject was: "What things will we teach kids from zero to 12 years old?" The trend has been to come up with a finite list of things kids should know and do. What's been concerning is how short these lists are. Some are as few as four points. Others are six or twelve points. The maximum I've seen is twenty-four points.

Now imagine that we were applying this philosophy to adults. We'd say, "Hey, you can come to our church, and in the next twelve years, you'll learn only twenty-four points. Yep, that's all you're getting! We'll repeat those twenty-four points over and over again, because that's what we feel you need." Do you think many adults would stay at that church?

Don't get me wrong, it's good to have a minimum list of things you'll cover; but don't limit kids. Don't insult their intelligence. For instance, if you allow kids to ask any spiritual question they'd like to ask, you'll find that they have hundreds and hundreds of questions, and they'll beg for them to be answered. (We'll show you how to unleash kids' questions in our "Life's Biggest Questions" series, which you can find on *KidsWantAnswers.com* as well). If you're teaching only twenty-four topics, then you're simply telling the kids that the church has very little to offer them.

In the end, we're called to make disciples. Now imagine the thousands of things the disciples learned while walking alongside Jesus for three years. I'm sure they absorbed more than twenty-four things a day! And we want to limit what we teach kids to twenty-four items—for twelve years? Don't be surprised when kids run away from church the moment they're old enough to tear the straightjacket off!

Disposable Tradition 5: The overuse of repetition. Here's the flow of most of today's children's services: Do some worship and some games, and then start the teaching. In the teaching, make one key point. Repeat this point into oblivion until kids are bored out of their skulls. Then have them chew on it some more in small groups. Keep repeating that one point until they're more than ready to run home.

The point? We're overusing repetition. We're so afraid that kids won't get it that we keep hammering the main point. How dumb do we think kids really are? Most of the teaching points we have can be absorbed in five minutes. What we do is throw two or three plot twists into our programs every week. It keeps the kids engaged and on their toes. We also have series, in which we start off saying: "Hey, kids, I'm not going to tell you what we're teaching today. You'll have to figure it out for yourself. Ready? Here we go!" The engagement is through the roof.

This—by the way—is how Jesus taught his parables. Note that Jesus didn't explain the meaning of many of his parables. In fact, He calls one of his parables the most important one. So important, in fact, that it was the key to understanding all others: *"Jesus said to them, 'Do you not understand this parable? Then how will you understand any of the parables?'"* (Mark 4:13, NIV). Since this parable was so important, he must have explained its meaning a hundred times, right? Nope. In fact, he never publicly did. He just told a story and then dropped the mic, leaving them guessing. Why? Maybe exactly because it was his most important parable! He wanted them to discover the meaning for themselves. A point self-discovered is much more valuable than a point you beat the audience over the head with. But you must trust the Holy Spirit a lot more if you want to teach the way Jesus did. To summarize: How do you know you're overusing repetition in your programs? Easy—kids don't maintain attention all the way through. How do you solve that? Plot twists, teaching points that deepen and grow, and self-exploration.

These were just five traditions we all can do without. I'm sure you can find many more. Each church has its unique traditions as well. Gather your team and let them put the unspoken traditions on the board. Look at which ones you can scratch, or even replace, with something fresh and creative.

Principle No. 3 – Call kids to a high commitment to Christ, not to baby steps.

Kids love a challenge. When they're challenged they'll grow fast. They'll grow so fast that our own spiritual growth can't keep up! But we often don't challenge kids. We're told to let them take baby steps because "they're only kids." But who are we to decide what kids can and cannot do? Let's leave that up to them, shall we?

If we lovingly challenge kids to the highest commitments to Christ, we'll be blown away. I've been blown away so many times. It's one of the most beautiful things of children's ministry. It may well be one of the reasons I do children's ministry. Kids don't have the fears and objections and excuses that adults do. They love to live up to the challenge.

Life itself will challenge kids. Sports will challenge them. School will challenge them. The draw of success will challenge them. Culture will challenge them. Why should we allow all these secondary things to challenge kids more than the church does? If we don't present the commitment challenges from God's Word, then who will? At least the church is a safe and loving environment where you won't be laughed at if you don't live up to a challenge. In the church, there are no sports teammates who laugh at you in the locker room; there is no grading system that tells you your performance is worthy of an *F*. The church is a place of love, and that's exactly why it's such a great place for kids to be challenged.

I don't need to tell you how to challenge in a loving and nonjudgmental way. You already know how to do that. I don't have to tell you to let each kid grow at their own speed. You already know how to do that, as well.

I once had a kid in my small group who had severe learning disabilities. He'd been diagnosed with a strong form of ADD too. (Trust me, no one needed to be told that he had been diagnosed. Let's just say, it was quite evident). He was placed in my small group and I told his mom how happy I was to have him. She was astonished. She explained about his ADD. I told her it was OK, that there were three other kids in the group who also had ADD and I would love having a fourth. Thinking I was a little crazy, the mom thanked me for welcoming her son, but also warned me that he shouldn't be asked to learn the Bible verses. I think she wanted to prepare me for disappointment, so I just nodded and said it would be all right. But you guessed it—I didn't do what she wanted. This is the church, not a restaurant where you get to request a customized order. It's up to the kids to decide how fast they want to grow, not the parents. It's not even up to me. I didn't say that, of course. So during the group time I lovingly challenged the boy to learn the verses, but only if he wanted to. I explained the benefit of knowing God's Word. He got it and wanted to learn the verses. In fact, he learned his verses each and every week and he was proud of it. After four weeks of this I bragged on him to his mom, telling her how awesome her son was. His mom ended up taking him out of the small group. Her son's incredible progress did not fit her picture of him. She wanted him to be a struggling kid. And too often, we are told as children's ministers to view kids that very way. The curriculum we buy doesn't challenge kids; it just teaches them one point a week. After all, kids are just helpless, cute little kittens in a basket, right?

Principle No. 4 – Have a high intolerance for "common ministry problems."

Ever heard of these common ministry problems?

- "Our volunteers keep standing in the back of the room."
- "The older boys are really ready for youth ministry."
- "Our sound-booth volunteers don't pay attention."
- "Kids get bored with a series after we're three weeks in."
- "The parent letter doesn't make it home."

They are so common that we can justifiably call them "common" ministry problems. They are the problems that never seem to get solved—until we realize we *can* solve them and then do something about it.

Just because every church seems to have these problems doesn't mean that we should accept them. If our solutions aren't working, then we need to try something different. We need to have a high intolerance toward accepting problems as unsolvable. Each of the problems I just listed can easily be solved.

Volunteers stand in the back for three reasons: (1) they get immersed in the program and feel stifled, (2) they aren't given a goal to accomplish while they stand in the back, and (3) they feel they're interrupting when they walk among the kids. With a little training, they won't stand in the back anymore.

When older kids goof off, put them on stage; let them serve. (There's more than one solution to this, but this is the first).

If your sound-booth volunteers don't pay attention, move the sound controls to the stage. Make them part of the program. Have your presenters banter back and forth with them, acting like they're talking with DJs on stage. Nobody goofs off when they're in the center of attention.

We can go down the list and attack every common problem with an encompassing solution. So can you. Start off by building up a high intolerance toward common ministry problems. For every problem there's a solution waiting to be found, and you'll find it.

You haven't reached the top yet, there's so much more mountain to climb. Enjoy the trip; the view is incredible.

Chapter 10

STYLE YOUR MINISTRY

Principle No. 5 – Completely adjust your style to the right target group.

EVERY CHURCH FEELS THE TENSION between insiders and outsiders, even though this tension should never exist. We all know that Jesus hung out with the outsiders, with tax collectors, prostitutes, and Samaritans. He called us to spread the good news, and we can't do that if we talk only to insiders. You already know that. But let's add another realization to this. The statistics we presented earlier show that even our kids who are insiders aren't exactly insiders. They're poised to walk away from church. In a sense, they're soon-to-be outsiders. A full 75 percent of them! So if we think and pray about this long and hard, we come to the following conclusions:

- If your first target group is the insiders, then you'll lose the outsiders and also 75 percent of the insiders.
- If your first target group is the outsiders, then you'll most likely gain outsiders—*and* you'll also reach the 75 percent of kids who are now insiders but soon-to-be outsiders. It's very unlikely that the remaining 25 percent of insiders will run away, either, because you'll have already trained them to engage outsiders for themselves.

Reread those two statements and let them sink in deeply. Which one is most like Jesus?

This goes right along with what Jesus said, *"For whoever wants to save his life will lose it, but whoever loses his life for My sake will save it"* (Luke 9:24, BSB). Let's view that verse in the context of children's ministry: "For whoever wants to save his children's ministry will lose it, but whoever loses his children's ministry for My sake will save it." We won't see God's growth unless we give his ministry back to him; not until we sacrifice it. Didn't Abraham have to put his own son on the altar? His Isaac—a true insider! But he made the sacrifice, and God spared Isaac and gave him back. Maybe you need to put "your" (it's really God's) children's ministry on the altar as well.

Jesus encouraged us to leave the ninety-nine sheep behind in order to find the one. That's quite a sacrifice. Imagine how hard it is! While searching for this one pesky sheep, the shepherd could hear the bleating of the ninety-nine over the hills. The longer the search, the more his inner voice must have been screaming: "Return! What are you doing? What if someone saw you like this? They'd say I'm a lousy shepherd!" But at the end of the story, the shepherd didn't have ninety-nine sheep. He had one hundred! How many would he have had if he didn't leave the ninety-nine behind? Would he only have ninety-nine sheep? My guess is ninety-eight. And the next day ninety-seven. And soon ninety-six. Do you see where this story is going? It's well on its way to describing today's children's ministry statistics, isn't it?

Just for fun, we began a YouTube channel for outsiders, and four years later it reached nearly 70,000 followers. We then did the same on Instagram and now reach more than 6,000 kids from all walks of life. The truth is that outsiders are more than happy to get to know you and the message God placed on your heart. All you have to do is present it in a way that helps them understand it and love it. And for the record, no, that does not mean you're watering down the message. It means exactly what you just read: that you present it in a way they can understand and love.

The most gifted communicator to ever walk this earth (I believe his name is Jesus?) started where people were. He spoke their language. He got on their level. He didn't believe he had to water down his message to reach them, but he did start where people were. This process of adjusting without compromising is best summed up in this verse: *"In addition to being a wise man, the Preacher also taught the people knowledge; and he pondered, searched out and arranged many proverbs"* (Eccl. 12:9, NASB). The pondering, searching out, and arranging is the same as changing your style to fit your target group.

There are two styles we need to change: your teaching style and your program's style. Your teaching style is the way you present. The program style is the form in which you present it. Content and form. Substance and label. Candy and wrapper. In this part we'll tackle the program style—the form, the wrapper. The teaching style will come in a later point.

So what style are today's kids craving? What speaks to kids in this day and age? For brevity's sake, we'll discuss the three biggest style changes. They're universal. Kids from Europe to Asia to North America will relate to them. These are in effect around the world. Once again, this program style is not based on theory or hopeful thinking. It's based on experience across more than twenty countries:

Style Change 1: Anything that's meant for kids isn't liked by kids.

If you try to reach elementary kids with kid stuff, you've already lost. Every entertainment industry, from film to music to gaming, already knows this. When we began to develop our videogame on the life of David, a high-profile games publisher contacted us. He happened to be a Christian. He told us not to turn it into a kid's game. He was right. Kids want stuff that's created for teenagers. It started with younger kids liking what their older siblings loved, but it's grown beyond that now. Media for kids has simply shrunk into a tiny sector. Todays' kids skip it and go straight to the teenage media franchises. This phenomenon is one of the biggest style differences between kids today and when you and I were kids. We've written extensively of why this has come about, and how it's not necessarily a bad thing.

However, when you look at most children's ministries you see well-meaning teams hopelessly trying to model their children's ministry after their favorite Disney cartoon era. We need to wake up from this. Not even Disney is putting that out anymore! Ask most kids what they like, and you'll find they are more into Marvel movies than Disney films. How about girls? Don't they want to become princesses? Yes, but the window of time that they want to has become radically short. Girls now read book series such as The Hunger Games and Twilight—teenage stories in which girls are powerful, strong, and independent. And boys? They play *Call of Duty, Modern Warfare,* and *Clash of Clans.* Kids currently love styles that are a bit darker and deal with real issues.

So how do you adjust your ministry to this new normal? It's quite simple, really. Adjust your style so you are no longer leading a children's ministry but a mini-youth ministry. You'll be running a youth ministry for kids, and it's a lot of fun to be involved in one. That counts for everything, from the feel of the room to the curriculum videos you play to the songs you sing. The whole experience should feel like youth stuff, look like youth stuff, sound like edgy youth stuff, but still be completely geared to kids. Throw out the primary colors, the high-pitched voices, the cartoony xylophone music that's under the teaching videos, the puppets, and the coloring pages, and replace them with edgier designs, relatable issue-based teaching, film-quality curriculum videos, self-discovery based teaching, and more. It's a trip!

When you turn your ministry in this new direction, you'll encounter many benefits. Not only will you reach both insider and outsider kids, but you'll also accomplish much more. More youth will come to serve, more dads will come to serve (parent involvement goes up because they don't have to slog through dorky kid stuff anymore), kid-to-kid evangelism goes up, and much, much more.

Style Change 2: Fast in, fast out.

Ever noticed that kids wiggle a lot more than adults? More and more adults are saying that kids have a short attention span. There's a lot of finger-pointing going on in that discussion. The big, bad technology devices and the entertainment media all are guilty. Parents are deemed guilty, as well. Sure, sure. Although this is partly true, let's focus on the solution, shall we?

We're hopelessly trying to figure out how to get kids to pay attention longer. Although there are more than five solutions to the attention problem, how about we turn the tables? What if we just shorten our program segments? We've come to call this "fast in, fast out." This means kids are quick to warm up to something. They don't need two minutes of guitar strumming to get in the mood to worship. As soon as the song plays, kids are ready to go. That's fast-in, fast-out. Kids are incredible at this, and we adults often forget they are. So, make the program segments shorter and have more of them instead of having a few long program segments. Your kids will love this style change. In the end, we say that they have a short attention span, but they say we like to drag things out. And aren't they kind of right?

Style Change 3: Have a high emphasis on quality media, but a low emphasis on show-performance.

I've been part of children's ministries that had incredible programming. I really value a well-oiled program, but I must admit that if I could go back in time, I would do things much differently. Sometimes we focus too much on the program (I've been guilty of that). If your program includes minute-to-minute scheduling, time cues, a never-ending fight against "dead time," full-blown rehearsals, and more, then you might want to rethink all that frantic effort. . If your ministry is focused a little too much on having a Disney or Theatre-like performance, allow me to relax you by showing the advantages of... well...relaxing a bit:

1. A high emphasis on performance stomps out most improvisation and leading of the Holy Spirit.
2. Getting the last 10 percent right takes more effort than doing the first 90 percent! Relax, you can do perfectly well without that final 10 percent.
3. You're not Disney. So stop trying to out-Disney Disney! Kid aren't at a theme park. They're at church.
4. Kids want a relationship with you. They don't want you to be someone who runs a show.
5. It's better to be real than programmed.
6. (Yes, there's more. But who's counting!) You'll never be able to let kids serve if everything has to be perfect. Your ministry should be not only for kids but also by kids. The same goes for adult volunteers. You'll want good teachers, but if your standards are too high, it'll be hard to slide new people in. Most people will need to grow into the role.
7. Performance-based ministries often require a ton of rehearsing and evaluating. That takes time away from the services, both before and after, which is valuable relationship-building time. Come on—kids would much rather have spontaneous conversations with you that make them feel like a million bucks than a perfect show.
8. (Yes, we're at no. 8, so let's go all the way!) God speaks through the kids as well. If everything is stage-based, you won't be able to allow God to speak through them.

Interaction decreases tremendously when you have to be on-the-minute to keep your schedule.

9. You'll never be perfectly on the minute, anyway, so why keep trying? Why all this frantic effort? Relax.
10. (We've reached double digits! We're really on to something here, aren't we?) Kids really aren't going to care if it's the house lights or the front spotlights that are on. And if microphone no. 3 doesn't go live exactly on time, just make a joke of it and talk louder.
11. Is there any love left for the poor guys and girls in the tech booth? Whenever I'm at any Christian event, a conference or children's ministry, I always befriend the audio team first. If they're stressed out, it tells me a whole lot about the true character of the organizers. The boot always comes down on the tech team first. So love these quiet geniuses.

Now, many children's ministries don't need these eleven points. They're just for ministries that may put too much emphasis on performance. Often times, the leadership has experience at theatre productions. Many other ministries need the opposite, and need to focus on quality more rather than less. You know which one you are.

The point of all of this is to encourage you to go for a relaxed 90 percent level of quality and not accept a lazy 40 percent quality level. The truth is, you should never be fine with your program being cheesy, having bad sound, poorly trained teachers, or projector bulbs that are burned out. When it comes to the media elements you use, go for the highest quality. We develop Hollywood-style videos because kids deserve the best. But we won't allow ourselves to stress out once we're on stage. Does that make sense? Go for the highest quality media but not the stressed-out show performance.

The best comparison (for me, obviously) is a food comparison. It's only healthy to cook with the highest-quality ingredients, but your ministry doesn't need to be a five-star restaurant. Just serve up a wonderful home-cooked meal with relational people around the table. Church is a family, not a performance. It's a household, not a show.

Style Change 4: Demolish predictability.

We already covered the fact that we overuse repetition. Repetition's cousin is predictability. When kids are young—under 7 years old—they love predictability. You'll see them jump up and down when they anticipate something fun is coming. For the elementary ages, the opposite is true. Predictability tunes them out.

Pop in any toddler TV series, and you'll see so much predictability you'll need a vacation before the series is over. Movies that aren't for toddlers, however, thrive on surprising you.

You know where I'm going with this. I don't even need to say it, do I? Yes, we all know it: Our programs follow the same structure each and every week. We buy a package that lasts us a year, and each lesson is structured the exact way. Our kids can already predict the next segment. No wonder they tune out and can't wait to go to youth ministry.

What's the solution? Keep kids on their toes. Unfortunately, this may mean you need to rewrite your curriculum every six or seven weeks. The series we have developed are all purposefully different. Each family of series has a different flow. The lessons are written in such a way that your volunteers can catch on quickly. The frequent changes won't burn them out. Quite the contrary; the changes keep them creative. In the end, it's easier for volunteers because the kids love to be surprised and engaging them is much easier.

Implementing these four style changes—a youth ministry for kids, fast-but-deep program segments, high-quality but low-stress style with variety—are incredibly fun to implement. There are many more, and I'm sure you and your team will find more as well.

You'll never be finished adjusting your ministry's style. Your community is constantly changing, and it's incredibly fun to keep discovering the style of your target group. Stay nimble and flexible by purposefully forgetting what worked last year. Always be learning and growing. Don't let experience trump innovation. We all like to say that working with kids keeps us young, right? Well, this is the part in which that happens. Here's to your never-ending youth!

Chapter 11

BUILD YOUR MINISTRY

Principle No. 6 – Include kids in leadership.

I'M OFTEN ASKED: "Should we let the youth help out? And what are they allowed to do, and at what age?" The answer to the first question is yes, and the second question is the wrong question (except when it's applied to the safety and security department). It's amazing that whenever we talk about youth serving, we like to ask, "What will we allow them to do?" But when we talk about adults serving, we say, "What's their giftedness?" Why don't we find out what our teenagers are gifted at rather than automatically thinking we need to police them? When they serve in line with how God shaped and gifted them, your security problems are cut in half. If you pair them with a good adult—Jedi-training-style—it cuts any issues in half again.

So that answers the youth question. We needed to answer that in order to take it a step further. How about letting the kids themselves serve? I'm not just talking about teenagers anymore, I'm talking about the kids who are in your room each week—those kids. Remember, kids aren't the Church of the future, they are today's Church. They don't just "attend" church to "learn." That sounds eerily close to the mission of a school system. You aren't leading a school; you're leading a children's ministry, a local church body. A church *of* kids, *for* kids, *with* kids, and *by* kids.

Now let's take this up a notch again: If you don't set an ambitious goal of having kids serve, then you'll let kids serve for a while, but then your program will sink back down to where it was: only adults will be doing the work. What if you set as your goal that half of all the serving roles must be fulfilled by kids? Actually, you can take it even further than that. What if *all* roles are fulfilled by kids, and the adults just coach and supervise?

Possible?

Absolutely.

I've encountered only two children's ministries in which the kids led everything. One is a ministry in Germany. The other is part of a megachurch in San Diego. Both thrived. Both were loved by the kids. The woman who led the German children's ministry told us, "Kids who serve at church stay at church." *Boom.* So there you have it—the antidote to children's-church decline. She nailed it in eight words. (Talk about German efficiency!)

Some ministries that tried this kids-in-leadership approach quickly abandoned it because it was too much work. They conducted full repetitions and evaluations with the kids. We use simpler formats. Remember, one of the style changes is shorter segments. Right? So, once you make your program segments shorter, you can give them away without needing to have kids practice much. Here are a few ways I've done this. It's deceptively simple:

1. Train one kid at a time. Pick a kid who attends regularly and meet with him or her separately to go over how to teach certain segments. Once they know how to teach a recurring segment, then they can teach those same segments in future lessons without your help.

2. Walk up to some courageous kids only minutes before the service and tell them they can do a segment if they want to. You should see their eyes grow big and their smile grow even bigger. I take them quickly through the segment and tell them I'll be onstage with them, with the secondary microphone, so they'll know I'm there if they need me. It's always been tons of fun. We banter back and forth and improvise and teach together.
3. Because that has been successful I've upped my game. I ask kids to help with upcoming segments *while* the program is going on. So, for example, when the teaching video is playing, I'll quietly ask a kid if he wants to do the next segment.
4. And because that too has gone well, I've upped my game yet again. I ask who in the audience wants to help teach *this* segment *right now*. If your program structure is loose and fun, and you're able to keep kids' attention while your trainee learns how to present, then it's a ton of fun and works every time.

This approach is interchangeable too. It works for more than just onstage speaking. Remember when, in Holland, I was asked to lead a children's ministry and then twelve of my leaders left? Well, I had only three left after that, and some weeks those three leaders couldn't make it. So I'd have thirty kids and, well, only me. Not a healthy long-term strategy, but boy did I learn a lot! Necessity breeds creativity. So I'd recruit kids to run the audio booth and handle the lights—while the service was going. For instance, I'd train kids how to do the lights while everybody listened to us. The trick to doing this is to turn it into an entertaining show for everybody. Here's an example of how I'd do it:

"Okay kids, before we start I need someone to run the lights. If you do it wrong, you get to blind me, if you do it right, you get a pat on the back. Either way you win. Who wants to learn how to do it? Okay, Theresa, you're it; come with me. See this button here?

Everybody else see it? Oh, of course not, only Theresa can see it because the other chumps are still in their chairs. Oh, wait, they can hear me? *Crud*! Anyway, this button is the full Damascus-style blinder, see? And this button is called 'House Lights'—maybe it kicks off a house party, I don't know—and this one is called 'Front Spots.' As we continue, I'll tell you which of the three buttons to press at what time. Don't fall asleep! Because if you do it wrong, we all get to laugh at you, so no pressure, *hmmkay*?"

All the kids would listen to that training because I'd simply do it over the microphone at the beginning of the service. The next week they'd all raise their hands to be the next one to do it. The more kids you pick, the more you've trained. Eventually you're not even worried about audio volunteers anymore.

Some might say this approach is perfect for small churches but not for megachurches, but that's not true. Just separate for kids the simple tasks from the complex ones. At megachurches, we simply forget that kids can serve really well and we require staff for everything. We also install complicated and expensive systems that then require adults to run them. So if you're building a new building or a new tech booth, focus on radical simplicity, or you'll lose the opportunity to let kids serve. (**Make a note:** Simplify some systems and leave the more complex ones for youth and adults. This way you can still pull off all the advanced stuff you want to do.)

So, to sum up principle 6:

Look for ways to involve kids; to have them teach, serve, or play in the band. If you work on making each service-opportunity simple, then you can teach kids in a way that doesn't tax your time. You can do it even while the service is underway!

Principle No. 7 – Focus the teaching on kids' felt needs and interests.

Some 80 percent of everything that happens at a weekend service is about the teaching. This goes for adults as well as for children. Most pastor-training sessions say that if the pastor wants to change things about his church, then he has to start by changing his teaching. The same goes for children's ministry. Sadly, in kid ministry we don't get to change our teaching much because it's decided by the curriculum we purchase, and curriculum publishers lose churches when they create content that's too innovative for the "mass market."

This doesn't change the fact that we HAVE to change the way we teach. You'll remember from the Gospels that the people who followed Jesus were constantly amazed at his teaching. Nobody spoke like him.

Here are a few of the many things we have changed about the way we teach (and this is obviously reflected in the curriculum we write):

Start with themes that kids will come for. No matter what you teach about, you can give your lesson a title and make that title sound inviting to kids. Why don't we ever do that in children's ministry? Youth ministries do it all the time. So does the Church, for adults. But we don't, because parents will bring their kids anyway. Right? Big mistake.

Say you're teaching on "humility" next week. That's the perfect opportunity to say, "Hey, kids, next week we're talking about one of the things you can do to be liked by many more people, and to make way fewer mistakes in life." (Obviously humility is the opposite of pride, and pride makes you blind). Do you think kids will be intrigued to attend church next week? Absolutely. Will they be more likely to bring their friends? Totally. Many of our series already give you titles you can advertise before you even run the series. But no matter what curriculum you use, you can find inviting titles and advertise them ahead of time. Base them on kids' spiritual interests, on their felt needs, on skills they'd like to learn—or just make it mysterious. Which brings us to the next point.

Embrace mystery and delayed answers. My friend and I once compared Christian films that were successful in the secular market with Christian films that were successful only in the Christian bubble. We came to a shocking realization: Catholic films have historically done way better than Protestant films. Look at *Braveheart, The Passion of the Christ, the Sound of Music, Schindler's List, Ben Hur,* and others. For days, we talked about how this could be. Among all the factors we considered, one stood out most: Catholic writers embrace mystery, while Protestant writers feel compelled to answer each question. Protestant movies, therefore, are quick to feel preachy.

As leaders, the same is true for our teaching. We are (rightfully) concerned that kids are given the right theology, which makes us Protestants quick to give answers. In fact, we answer questions that kids haven't even asked yet! In many ways this is opposite to Jesus' teaching style. He told parables to which he even "forgot" to give the answers. He'd simply end with the mysterious statement: *"He who has ears, let him hear"* (Matthew 13:9, BSB). He spoke in mysteries so often that it bugged his disciples: "His disciples said, "See, NOW you are speaking plainly and without figures of speech." (John 16:29, BSB; emphasis mine).

In other trainings, we've spoken about how to help kids to first ask questions, how to raise their interest, how to delay the answer, how to help them find the answers themselves, and how to send them home with even more questions, allowing them to constantly be growing. In our training on *5 New Ways to Lead Kids to Christ* (it's on the website), we show you how we helped kids to grow a spiritual appetite, simply by asking them deep questions without answering those questions for them. Kids who were completely disinterested in Christ would be more than ready to accept him nine weeks later. When you delay answers, you allow the Holy Spirit to work in their hearts. But it takes a lot of trust in God to let kids walk out the door with unanswered questions.

- **Start with the questions kids are asking.** How many lessons out there start with questions kids ask? Hardly any. We love to go through the Bible chronologically, or speak about how kids are God's masterpieces and how God loves them. Those are all good things. But we also need lessons that start with the questions kids ask. For five years we gathered all the questions kids ask and wrote series that answer them (delayed answers, mind you!).
- **Let discovery truly be discovery.** We all love such words as "quest," "journey," "discovery," and "adventure." But rarely does any children's ministry lesson actually take kids on a quest, adventure, or journey. We just teach and teach and teach. True self-discovery means you let go of control. It means kids might get things out of the Bible that are biblical but aren't the topics you meant to teach on that week. If you truly would like for kids to go on a discovery, you'll have to let go. Are you willing to?
- In describing the New Testament Church, the Apostle Paul seems to say that anybody who has heard from Christ can say something about it in church. What if we allowed kids to be the Church? What if we accepted them as the Church? Could they share what they discovered? Once you allow this, you'll first be sweating profusely, hoping it all goes well. But once you learn to facilitate what's going on, it becomes an incredible and grateful ride. You'll be brought to tears when God speaks through the little ones. You'll get to praise and highlight the wisdom that comes from their mouths. You'll be astonished when mature kids lovingly correct kids who are just starting out. Each week, you'll never know what to expect. Adventure has truly become adventure.

Principle No. 8 – Teach the Bible in such a way that kids can teach others.

When I was just starting out with children's ministry and would notice kids who were ready to accept Christ, I'd take them to a quiet place and lead them to Jesus. As time went on, I switched strategies. Instead of taking them aside, I'd keep them with their friends. Others would come along, wondering what we were talking about, and they'd join in and accept Christ as well. Later I took this even further by refusing to lead kids to Christ. Instead, if I noticed that a kid was ready, I'd call on any kid who was near us and have that kid lead the other one to Christ (yes, even if that kid didn't yet know how to. I'd just tell them step by step how to do it).

This approach changed everything for me. It also changed the way I teach—which is based on this realization: Kids will teach other kids the same way they were taught. They'll tell it the way they heard it. So if you let them hear it in a way they can use to spread it, you've just made them a more effective teacher.

Does that make sense? So here's the kicker; if you teach it in a way they can use to teach others, they'll automatically spread it easier. I'll make that more practical: instead of just teaching them something new, teach them how to teach something new. Even if you're giving them completely new information, tell them about the new tidbits by acting as if they're experts and they're teaching others.

Here's an example:

Here's the traditional way of teaching: "Hey kids, I have something great to tell you. Which one of you ever wonders, 'If God's real, why is he invisible?' Well, let me tell you...." This is first-level teaching. It's you telling them. Let's take it up a notch in the next example:

"Hey kids, if anyone ever comes up to you and asks, 'If God is out there, why is he invisible?' what would you answer that person? What could you possibly tell them? What's an answer he could live with? And what answer do you give yourself if you're asking the same question? Well, let me tell you what you could tell him...."

In the second example, kids are automatically thinking with you because they want to help this imaginary person. I can guarantee you that they don't know why God is invisible, but even though they don't know yet, they'll soon know both the answer and how to tell others the answer!

One of the common problems we have in Western society is that we think sequentially. We think in steps. We make steps out of things that can easily be done all at once. We often think that we first need to teach kids for themselves, and then show them how to teach others. This method defeats itself. Kids will teach others something the same way they first learned it. You can't undo the first impression with a second. Instead, make part of their first impression how to teach others. Imagine if all Christians were led to accept Christ in a way that they could lead others to Christ! How many Christians would be great at evangelism then?

This approach also solves the invitation problem. How often have you encouraged kids to invite their friends to church? Often, right? This is great—and please keep doing so—but the truth is, although many kids would love to bring their friends to church, many of their friends will never come. If their friends grow up in Muslim, Buddhist, or Jewish families, they often won't come. So we have to train kids not only to invite and bring friends to church, but also to BE the Church to their friends. Many churches don't train kids for this because it doesn't grow the church. It doesn't bring in new people. But it advances God's kingdom, and that's more important than the size of a local church.

In our curriculum you'll often see the teaching written out. We do this to give you an example of how to teach. In many cases, you'll be told to teach in this secondary form. We've never explained why we do this, but now you know.

Principle No. 9 – Teach truth while contrasting it with the ideas of culture.

We've all heard about apologetics. Youth ministries teach apologetics quite often, but children's ministries are lagging behind a little (yes, we've already covered that fact, haven't we?). But we can do more than just catch up; we can take things even further.

See, apologetics often is a bit narrow. It simply puts truth next to lies and that's about it. Many apologetic teachers believe they help their pupils to evangelize, but they don't even come close to succeeding in the evangelistic arena. Instead, they just provide students with knowledge so they can win arguments against atheists and other thinkers.

Sadly, arguments rarely win hearts. Arguments just win arguments. It's been said that "a person convinced against his will is of the same opinion still." You can't argue people into heaven. Arguments make people angry, and surrendering to Christ requires a surrendered heart, not an angry heart.

So we go a little further and teach kids what we jokingly call "apologetics plus," or "loving apologetics." It's good to add some loving apologetics to any of your teaching.

Here's how it works:

After you teach kids something new, you say: "Now, some people who don't yet know about Jesus might believe something different. They would say X-Y-Z. Is that true?" Allow the kids to answer. If the kids are really good, throw in some more secular arguments and allow the kids to dispel them. After that, take them deeper by saying: "Now, let's say that you have a friend who believes X-Y-Z. If you just tell him he's wrong, is he going to be convinced?" Allow kids to answer. Then say: "No, you have to be loving. So I need you to think deeply for a second. What I'm going to ask from you is this: "How can you teach him the truth in a way that he would actually like? What would you say?" You can help them step by step to find a loving way to spread the truth. I've gone as far as to explain to kids exactly WHY some people choose to believe lies and to address the WHY behind the lie, not the lie itself. You'll be surprised at how good and wise kids can be in the loving apologetics department. In fact, you might learn a thing or two from them. I know I have (but then again, I'm blonde, so it's not too hard for kids to outsmart me!).

Chapter 12

TURN YOUR MINISTRY INSIDE OUT

Principle No. 10 – Give your ministry an outward focus and help kids to be leaders in their world

THIS POINT IS RELATED TO the last one, but it is also inherently different. From your purpose statement to your ministry culture, every area of your ministry should be focused on one truth: we're here to reach the kids of our community and make them disciples. Everybody involved in the ministry needs to know about this, even the kids themselves. Evangelism is always the first thing to be neglected.

But advertising your goal and putting it everywhere is not enough. It won't go anywhere unless it is implemented. Here are three ways you can do that:

1. Turn your weekend services inside out (See our book and training *10 Ways to Explode Your Children's Ministry*).
2. Throw community-outreach events and other similar events. This is a great approach, and we'll cover it in other trainings.

3. Train kids to reach their friends.

The kids may be your strongest allies in reaching the community, so speak about it often. Train them well. And for heaven's sake—quite literally for heaven's sake—do not tell them that evangelism is scary. Many kids are oblivious to the fact that adults are scared of evangelism. If you talk about evangelism, keep your own fear out of it. Don't be like the mom who fearfully holds her kid's hands when she takes him to the dentist. Her fear transfers to her son and the boy becomes scared of the dentist too. But if the mom acts like she has no fear whatsoever, the kid might just enjoy his dentist visit. Be well aware: you could give kids fears for life that aren't necessary. On the other hand, you could also give them skills for life that serve them well.

By training them this way, you help kids to become leaders outside the Church. It's not enough for kids to be leaders inside the Church (see Principle 6); it's also incredibly rewarding to help them to be leaders in their community. We often understate the importance of Christians who are being salt and light in the community. But the truth is, your kids are called to be leaders not just in the church but in the world as well: *"Seek the peace and prosperity of the city to which I have carried you....Pray to the Lord for it, because if it prospers, you too will prosper"* (Jeremiah 29:7, NIV).

Principle No. 11 – Move from external motivation to internal motivation.

There are two ways to motivate kids: external motivation and internal motivation. External motivation is when you motivate them with prizes, reward systems, and so on. They'll be motivated as long as the stimulus is there.

Internal motivation means helping a kid to become self-motivated, to get closer to God, to learn more about Christ, to be involved in church, and so on.

External motivation is not always bad, but it's limited. It's shallow. Sometimes it adds a great boost to the program. But when you start to use it regularly, you begin to train kids to after for the prize, not pursue spiritual growth. Always use external motivators to move kids toward internal motivation. You do this by retiring the external systems over time. Here's an example of how (and why) I retired a system:

A ministry I once led used a balloon system as an external motivator. We started with three balloons. If kids were not paying attention, a balloon would be popped. If all three balloons were popped, that team would not receive candy at the end. This system served its purpose to keep kids from goofing off. But it had a flaw too. You might have guessed it: after the third balloon was popped, the team was off the hook. There would be nothing left to lose, so they'd behave like animals. To counteract this, no leader would ever pop the third balloon. But of course the kids weren't dumb and knew what the leaders were doing, so they'd goof off regardless. As you can tell, the kids learned how to "hack" the system. They'd behave based on the system, not based on common decency. So I had to retire the system.

It took three or four weeks to get the regular kids used to the fact that there now would be neither a reward nor a punishment. To behave, they'd have to rely instead on their own internal motivation. Once kids were used to this—and believe me, it took some gifted teachers to implement it, teachers who could maintain control—the menacing behavior stopped. There was no more system to hack, no game to be played.

Even though that is an example of kids' behavior, the same goes for kids' interest in Christ. If kids learn their verses just to get a reward, they will stop learning them once they grow out of the ministry. But if they learn verses because they've clearly seen the benefit of God's Word—they've seen it help them in their daily lives, so they actually want to learn verses—then they'll keep doing it throughout their lives. Internal motivation is what you're after.

Sometimes you need an external motivation system to start off with things. But treat these systems like scaffolds; they're meant to be retired soon. Other times we feel that we need external motivation systems but we really don't. Instead, we can start off with internal motivation right away. Why take two steps if you can reach your destination with one?

Principle No. 12 – Don't believe the programs will do the work for you.

I once had a meeting I was really nervous about. One of the best-known children's pastors in the nation wanted to have lunch with me. Obviously, I was intimidated—I looked up to the man and the ministry he led. But that wasn't why I was nervous. It was because he'd asked me to survey his weekend services for two months and tell him what he should change. He wanted me to critique his work.

That alone was intimidating, but what was worse was that I had learned so much from his ministry while I was observing it that I was only full of praise. I had no idea what should be improved. The programs were amazing. But I knew he wouldn't be interested in praise. He already knew what was good. He wanted to know what should improve.

So he asked me the question, and I deflected. He was smart enough to notice that I'd done and brought the conversation to a halt. He asked me again. There was no way out. I had to answer.

Consciously, I wasn't aware of a way to better his ministry. But nonetheless something about it was bugging me—I just couldn't put my finger on it. God was stirring my heart, but I didn't know what he was trying to tell me. So I prayed a quick prayer and decided to answer from the gut. I was just going to speak from the feeling God had put in my heart. This was a bit dangerous, I knew, because speaking that way meant that I'd have no filter.

I took a deep breath and then heard myself say: "There's nothing wrong with the weekend program. It's great. What's wrong is that you're expecting the program to do the work. The leaders don't interact with the kids enough. They're not getting the friendships that they need in order to become true disciples. Disciples aren't being made."

Suddenly, it was completely quiet. At our table, at least. Slowly, a smile of appreciation formed on the man's face. He had received honesty and he was mature enough to accept it and deal with it. Over the coming year I worked closely with the coordinators of each age group in his children's ministry to raise up volunteers who would, on purpose, have no programming tasks. They were called "roamers." Their job was to have spiritual conversations with kids before, after, and—yes—during the service! They'd go from open chair to open chair, sit down, and then talk with the kids to their left and right. We told the kids that they could always talk with a leader, at any point in the program. There was no time when they couldn't talk with a leader.

The leading verse we used for this initiative was a little obscure passage in Nehemiah 8. Ezra the scribe would read the Law aloud to the people, and while he did, the Levites would walk around and explain what the Law meant, *"so that the people understood the reading"* (Nehemiah 8:8). That's one of the things roamers did. But they did much more.

Roamers were tasked to assess where kids were spiritually. They were tasked to build relationships, attend to kids' needs, answer questions, ask questions (as you saw before, this is most important!), raise kids' spiritual interests, explain the story of the Bible (there's a drawing we use that shows the entire story of the Bible), meet their parents, report great stories, lead huddle groups, give out Bibles, write encouraging notes and letters, and much more.

You get the point: roamers were shepherds to the kids on the weekend. We'll soon have a more in-depth training on all the incredibly fun things roamers get to do. We'll keep you up to date through the *KidsWantAnswers.com* newsletter, which you can find on the site. Implementing this system will change your ministry completely. If the teaching portion is 50 percent effective, then roamers will be make up the other 50 percent. I firmly believe that roamers double the effect of your ministry.)

As you probably know, deep relationships are built in small groups. But small groups where deeper relationships can be formed are often closed off to new people for periods of time so that the kids feel safe to share and go deep. This is great, but not for new kids. Many new kids come only on weekends, but they crave the personal environment as well. Roamers can fill the void between the weekend services and the small groups. And in doing so, they make the takeaway from services twice as effective.

IT'S ABOUT COMPASSION, NOT AMBITION

When you desire to reach many kids for Christ, people in your church may not understand. Some are great at ministering to insiders but have a hard time accepting outsiders. Even though they read the same Bible you read, they may emphasize things other than the Great Commission and the Great Commandment.

Some misinterpret how things work by saying that you can't possibly "go deep" with a large ministry. They'll say, "The church needs to be unified before we reach out," which is a goal so vague that it'll never be accomplished. Others might become jealous of you the moment you cast new vision and work against you without reason. Others may attack your character and say you're just an ambitious person. They'll use the word "ambition" like it's a self-glorifying disease. (Apparently, any ambition is good except if it's for God's kingdom!)

But you and I both know you're not in kidmin because you're ambitious. It's not about your ambition. It's not about any of us at all, in fact. It's about God's love for the lost. That's why you're in ministry. It's God's love that compels you, that makes your heart beat faster, that makes you run fast and steady, that makes you run after God, no matter how old you are.

Our prayer for you as you start to take the principles we've given you in this book and put them into action is that God will give you a double dose of his love for the lost, and then double it again. Let him give you so much love that your heart feels like it will explode! Because God is love, and his love is the only thing that'll change things on our little broken planet.

I often pray for God to break my heart again and again. It needs to be broken repeatedly because it will harden by itself. It will grow cold when it's on autopilot. I encourage you to do the same—give God permission to break your heart.

Acts 13:36 tells us that David served God's purpose in his generation. May the same be said about you after your life is over. When the Bible says, "his generation," it means all the people who were alive during David's lifetime. The Bible doesn't delineate between a Boomer or a Gen-Xer or a Millennial. Those are just social divisions created by marketers.

As the Church, we're here to serve everyone who's alive while we are. That's *our* generation. And our generation includes kids. They're as much a part of this generation as we are.

May there be no division between us.

MORE BY TORNADOTWINS

S.O.S.

How to stay close to God

KIDSWANTANSWERS.COM/SOS

This series is specifically designed for the *invited kid, the XP kid, the buzz kid.*

Create a baffling week-to-week children's ministry experience with this seven-week series for ages 6-12.
Kids will follow the story of Joey, who gets stranded at a deserted Island. This hilarious story ends with a cliff hanger each week, keeping kids in suspense of what will happen next week, while teaching them the essential habits any Christian needs in order to stay close to God.

MORE BY TORNADOTWINS

David 1 & 2

How to be a leader

KIDSWANTANSWERS.COM/RESOURCES

Both of these 5-week series help kids to become deeply immersed in the life of David.

With cutting edge full-feature animations, you will take kids through the book of 1st Samuel; from when we first hear of David to when he's crowned king over Judah. They'll learn what made David such a great leader that God called him "a man after God's own heart."

Kids can even unlock a videogame of David's life and give their feedback to the twins, who are developing the game of David!

These series have been a vision for over 10 years, and the twins are incredibly excited to share it with you.

For more TornadoTwins curriculum, videogames, books and movies, visit:

KIDSWANTANSWERS.COM

CPSIA information can be obtained
at www.ICGtesting.com
Printed in the USA
LVOW11s0122080317
526486LV00002B/270/P

9 781943 294497